Acknowledgements

The compilers and the publishers wish to thank the following for permission to use copyright material:

Martin Secker & Warburg Ltd., for *Last Snow* and *A Windy Day* by Andrew Young, from 'Complete Poems'.

The Literary Executor of Leonard Clark, for *First Primrose*, *In June*, *July Night*, *August Ends*, *Leaves and Fires*, *Corn and Nuts*, *Harvests* and *Hallowe'en*, from 'Collected Poems and Verses for Children', published by Dennis Dobson, and for *Fog in November*, from 'Four Seasons', published by Dennis Dobson.

Abelard-Schuman Ltd., for *A Spike of Green* by Barbara Baker.

Jean Kenward, for *Frog Spawn*, *Snow*, *Frozen Stiff*, *Windmill Jack* and *Bonfire*.

Harper & Row, Publishers, Inc. and World's Work Ltd., for the text of *Sunning* by James S. Tippett, from 'Crickety Cricket! The Best-Loved Poems of James S. Tippett'. Originally published in 'A World to Know' by James S. Tippett. Copyright 1933 by Harper & Row, Publishers, Inc. Renewed 1961 by Martha K. Tippett.

Hubert Nicholson, as Literary Executor, and Autolycus Publications, for *A Hot Day* by A.S.J. Tessimond, from 'Not Love Perhaps'.

Michael Joseph Ltd., for *A Dragonfly* by Eleanor Farjeon, from 'Silver Sand and Snow'.

Western Publishing Company Inc., for *August* by Michael Lewis, from 'Golden Treasury of Poetry'. © 1959 Western Publishing Company Inc.

John Smith, for *In August*, from 'The Early Bird and the Worm', published by Burke Publishing Co. Ltd.

Macmillan Publishing Co. Inc., for *Something Told the Wild Geese* by Rachel Field. Copyright 1934 by Macmillan Publishing Co. Inc., renewed 1962 by Arthur S. Pederson.

Mrs. A.M. Walsh, for *Sweet Chestnuts*, from 'The Roundabout by the Sea' by John Walsh.

The Executors of the W.H. Davies Estate and Jonathan Cape Ltd., for an extract from *The One Singer*, and for *The Fog*, both from 'The Complete Poems of W.H. Davies'.

Evans Brothers Ltd., for *Colour* by Adeline White, *Rainy Nights* by Irene Thompson and *Four Scarlet Berries* by Mary Vivian, from 'The Book of a Thousand Poems', compiled by J. Murray Macbain.

Curtis Brown Ltd., for *Winter Morning* by Ogden Nash. Copyright © 1961, 1962 by Ogden Nash.

The Literary Trustees of Walter de la Mare and The Society of Authors as their representative, for *The Snowflake*, *Snow*, *The Ride-by-Nights* and *Please to Remember* by Walter de la Mare.

Mrs. Iris Wise and Macmillan, London and Basingstoke, for *White Fields* by James Stephens, from 'Collected Poems'.

Vernon Scannell, for *Death of a Snowman*, from 'The Apple Raid and Other Poems'.

Penguin Books Ltd., for *Winter Days* by Gareth Owen, from 'Gareth Owen: Salford Road' (Kestrel Books, 1979), p. 65. Copyright © 1971, 1974, 1976, 1979 by Gareth Owen.

Dennis Dobson, Publishers, for *Rain* by Spike Milligan, From 'A Dustbin of Milligan', and *Granny* by Spike Milligan, from 'Silly Verse for Kids'.

Methuen & Co. Ltd., for *Rain* by Brian Lee, from 'All Sorts of Poems', edited by Ann Thwaite, published by Magnet Books.

Curtis Brown Ltd. on behalf of James Kirkup, for *Thunder and Lightning*.

The Hamlyn Publishing Group Ltd., for *In the Rain* by René Cloke, from 'A Posy of Little Verses'.

Oxford University Press, for *Mrs. Golightly* and *Fireworks*, from 'The Blackbird in the Lilac' by James Reeves (1952), for *W is for Witch* by Eleanor Farjeon, from 'The Children's Bells', and for *The Guy* by Robert C. Holmes, from 'Every Man Will Shout', edited by Roger Mansfield and Isobel Armstrong (1964).

William Heinemann Ltd., for *The Wind* from 'The Wandering Moon' by James Reeves.

Atheneum Publishers Inc., for *Wind Song* by Lilian Moore (Copyright © 1966 by Scholastic Magazines Inc.) in 'I Feel the Same Way'. Copyright © 1967 by Lilian Moore (New York: Atheneum, 1967).

Stanley Cook, for *The Wind* and *Bonfire Night*, from 'Come Along', published by the author, 600 Barnsley Road, Sheffield, S5 6UA.

Angus & Robertson (UK) Ltd., for an extract from 'A Song of Wind' by Will Lawson, from 'Chosen for Children'.

Faber & Faber Ltd., for *Gale Warning*, from 'Collected Poems' by Michael Roberts, and for *Harvest Home*, from 'Collected Poems' by Herbert Read.

Harcourt Brace Jovanovich Inc., for *Fog*, from 'Chicago Poems' by Carl Sandburg, copyright 1916 by Holt, Rinehart & Winston Inc.; copyright 1944 by Carl Sandburg.

Douglas Gibson, for *Mist* and *Fireworks*.

Miss Penelope Rieu, for *The Hippopotamus's Birthday* by E.V. Rieu.

The Society of Authors and Miss Pamela Hinkson, for *August Weather* by Katharine Tynan.

Marnie Pomeroy, for an extract from *Hallowe'en*, from 'Poems for Seasons and Celebrations'.

Methuen & Co. Ltd., for an extract from *Mixed Brews* by Clive Sansom, from 'The Golden Unicorn'.

James Nimmo Britton, for *Space Travellers*.

Harper & Row, Publishers, Inc., for the text of *The Witches' Ride*, from 'The Rose on my Cake' by Karla Kuskin. Copyright © 1964 by Karla Kuskin.

James Gibson, for *Fireworks* by Elizabeth Clare.

Laurie Lee, for an extract from *Christmas Landscape*.

Blackie & Son Ltd., for *Silver Bells* by Hamish Hendry.

E.P. Dutton, Publishers, for *Christmas Eve*, from 'Feelings and Things' by Edna Kingsley Wallace. Copyright 1916 by E.P. Dutton & Co. Inc. Renewal, 1944, by Edna Kingsley Wallace.

William Collins Sons & Co. Ltd., for *The Carol Singers* by Margaret G. Rhodes.

Peter Hancock, for *Poor Decorations*.

Lillian Boucher, for *Frost*.

We have been unable to trace the copyright owners of the following poems and should be pleased to hear from them or their heirs and assigns. In the meantime, we venture to include:

The Seasons by P.E. Bath; *Only the Wind Says Spring* by Helen Janet Miller; *April* by Ted Robinson; *Autumn* by Florence Hoatson; *Leaf-fall* by E.H. Ray; *Autumn* by T.E. Hulme; *A Rainy Day* by Andrew West; *Storm* by R.N. Bartlett; *The Fog* by F.R. McCreary; *November Mist* by Bernard W. Martin; *Firework Night* by Eric Simpson; *The Christmas Party* by Adeline White.

Contents

BGBQ £5·90 m

Poetry Plus

Book One

A Diary of Poems

Written and compiled by

B.R. Marney
M. Hussamy
A.N. Ashton
S.M. Parle

Illustrated by Margaret Sherry

Schofield & Sims Ltd.   Huddersfield.

0 7217 0431 X

First Printed 1982
Reprinted 1983 (twice), 1984, 1986, 1990

Poetry Plus is a series of five books:

Book 1   0 7217 0431 X
Book 2   0 7217 0432 8
Book 3   0 7217 0433 6
Book 4   0 7217 0434 4
Book 5   0 7217 0435 2

Foreword

One of the aims of *Poetry Plus* is to stimulate children to write
their own poems. To encourage this, each section begins with
a series of thought-provoking questions and relevant vocabulary.
In addition, each provides ideas for inter-related topic work
which should promote higher reading skills and simple research.

Poetry Close-up pages consider individual poems and related
interest areas.

The poems have been carefully selected for variety and quality
and are grouped so that immediate interests and enthusiasms can
be pursued.

We hope that children will enjoy reading and listening to the
poems in *Poetry Plus* and that the series will encourage them to
write creatively.

Typeset in England by H Charlesworth & Co Ltd, Huddersfield
Printed in England by Stott Bros. Ltd., Halifax

Contents

Contents

Section Three: **Special Days and Festivals**

The Seasons

The Seasons

Leafless trees
Heavy seas
Snow and rime
Resting time
   That's Winter.

Days less chill
Winds less shrill
Waking flowers
Mellow showers
   That's Spring.

Flowers in crowds
Absent clouds
New mown hay
A longer day
   That's Summer.

Golden sheaves
Falling leaves
Birds in flight
Skies less bright.
   That's Autumn.

P.E. BATH

Spring

"Now the buds and leaves are seen
Now the fields are fresh and green"

In this section you will find some poets' thoughts
on spring. Read the poems and think about these
questions on this season of new life and activity.

What does spring make you think of?

.... warmer and longer days .... blustery winds ....
April showers.

Why is spring a special time for living things?

.... Think of — first flowers .... fragrant blossom ....
birds busily nesting .... newborn lambs.

If you wish to write your own poem, these words
may help you.

fledgling	burst	gust	gentle	invigorating	billow	emerge
unfurl	verdant	frolic	fleecy	shades	leap	excite
awaken	lush	wonder	fresh	appear	timid	
mild	clusters	stir	rainbow	gambol	shoot	

Spring Spotlight

Find out about birds in spring ....
.... Make a list of birds which arrive in this country in
spring .... Where do they come from?
.... Choose one bird and make a detailed study of it
with sketches.
Write about where it nests .... the colour, size
and number of eggs it lays .... the differences
between male and female .... what it eats ....
whether it migrates.

If you turn to page 14 you will find some questions
on the poems themselves and some more things to do.

Only the Wind Says Spring

The grass still is pale, and spring is yet only a wind stirring
    Over the open field.
There is no green even under the forest leaves.
    No buds are blurring
    The pencil sketch of trees. No meadows yield
The song of larks, nor the buzz of bees conferring.
Only the wind says spring. Everything else shouts winter;
    The whitened beards of grass,
The shrivelled legs of corn with their trousers flapping,
    The year-old cuts in the root of the sassafras;
A spruce-cone empty of seeds, the scales unwrapping
    Open to dryness, last year's withered peach,
A stiff tomato-vine begun to splinter,
    The crones of milkweed talking each to each.

The earth stands mute, without a voice to sing.
But the wind is saying spring.

HELEN JANET MILLER

Last Snow

Although the snow still lingers
Heaped on the ivy's blunt webbed fingers
And painting tree-trunks on one side,
Here in this sunlit ride
The fresh unchristened things appear,
Leaf, spathe and stem,
With crumbs of earth clinging to them
To show the way they came
But no flower yet to tell their name,
And one green spear
Stabbing a dead leaf from below
Kills winter at a blow.

ANDREW YOUNG

Winter and Spring

But a little while ago
All the ground was white with snow;
Trees and shrubs were dry and bare,
Not a sign of life was there;
Now the buds and leaves are seen,
Now the fields are fresh and green,
Pretty birds are on the wing,
With a merry song they sing!
There's new life in everything!
How I love the pleasant spring!

ANON.

April

So here we are in April, in showy, blowy April,
  In frowsy, blowsy April, the rowdy, dowdy time;
In soppy, sloppy April, in wheezy, breezy April,
  In ringing, stinging April, with a singing, swinging
    rhyme!

The smiling sun of April on the violets is focal,
  The sudden showers of April seek the dandelions out;
The tender airs of April make the local yokel vocal,
  And he raises rustic ditties with a most melodious
    shout.

So here we are in April, in tipsy, gypsy April,
  In showery, flowery April, the twinkly, sprinkly days;
In tingly, jingly April, in highly, wily April,
  In mighty, flighty April with its highty-tighty ways!

The duck is fond of April, and the clucking chickabiddy
  And other barnyard creatures have a try at carolling;
There's something in the air to turn a stiddy kiddy giddy
  And even I am forced to raise my croaking voice
    and sing.

TED ROBINSON

First Primrose

I saw it in the lane
One morning going to school
After a soaking night of rain,
The year's first primrose,
Lying there familiar and cool
In its private place
Where little else grows
Beneath dripping hedgerows,
Stalk still wet, face
Pale as Inca gold,
Spring glistening in every delicate fold.
I knelt down by the roadside there,
Caught the faint whiff of its shy scent
On the cold and public air,
Then got up and went
On my slow way,
Glad and grateful I'd seen
The first primrose that day,
Half yellow, half green.

LEONARD CLARK

A Spike of Green

When I went out
The sun was hot
It shone upon
My flower pot.

And there I saw
A spike of green
That no one else
Had ever seen!

On other days
The things I see
Are mostly old
Except for me.

But this green spike
So new and small
Had never yet
Been seen at all!

BARBARA BAKER

12

Frog Spawn

The Rooks

The rooks are building on the trees;
   They build there every spring:
'Caw, caw,' is all they say,
   For none of them can sing.

They're up before the break of day,
   And up till late at night;
For they must labour busily
   As long as it is light.

And many a crooked stick they bring,
   And many a slender twig,
And many a tuft of moss, until
   Their nests are round and big.

'Caw, caw.' Oh, what a noise
   They make in rainy weather!
Good children always speak by turns,
   But rooks all talk together.

AUNT EFFIE
(JANE EUPHEMIA BROWN)

Down in the pond
   there's a swirling
a heaving
   a bobbing
      and plopping,
and blobs
   of stuff
      that is swishy
and sloppy
   and splishy
are swooling about there
   in swabs.

Down in the pond
   there's a thingmebob
      croaking
and flipping
   and floating,
      and soon
there'll be spickles
   and speckles
      and dark, dotty freckles
blown up
   in a jelly
      balloon!

JEAN KENWARD

Poetry Close-up

1. In the poem called 'Only the Wind Says Spring',
   there is a sentence which makes us think that the
   trees have no leaves. Can you find it?
   How does the writer describe the grass so that we
   know it's frosty?

   In the same poem there are some difficult words.
   Can you find out, for example, what 'sassafras' is
   and why it has cuts in its root?

2. In the poem called 'Winter and Spring', what does
   the poet love about spring?
   He writes about birds singing. Do you know why
   they sing?

3. What does Ted Robinson mean by 'sprinkly days'
   in the poem called 'April'?

4. If you look at the poem called 'The Rooks', you
   will see that the poet says that none of the rooks
   can sing. Can you explain why she said that?

5. Write a story in which you imagine you are an
   animal waking up in spring after your winter
   sleep. Describe what you see, feel, hear, smell
   and do.

Other Things To Do

. . . . What can you discover about germination?
Perhaps you could bring some seeds and cuttings
to grow in the class-room. Keep a daily record of
their progress.

. . . . Find out about the life cycle of the frog.

. . . . Describe any new life you have seen, perhaps a
puppy. What did it look like? How did it move?
What noises did it make?

Summer

"When the heat of the summer
Made drowsy the land."
In this section you will find some poets'
thoughts on summer. Read the poems and think
about these questions on the hot, lazy days of
summer.

How does the weather affect you in summer?

. . . . Think of — enjoyable, sunny days . . . . warm, light
nights . . . . sun-tans and blisters . . . .
sweltering afternoons . . . . sudden
thunderstorms . . . . dry throats.

Why is it a season of exciting colours?

. . . . Think of — bright flowers . . . . lush, green fields
. . . . clear blue skies.

What do you look forward to in summer?

. . . . Think of — picnics . . . . school holidays . . . .
day trips . . . . golden beaches.

If you wish to write your own poem, these words
may help you.

sizzle	sultry	hazy	fragrant	stroll	browse
stifling	oppressive	idle	scent	lifeless	sticky
humid	dazzle	cloudless	aroma	amble	sleepy
scorched	lazy	languid	drought	drowsy	indolent

Summer Sun

Is the Sun a star?
. . . . Find out what the Sun is made of . . . . how far away
it is . . . . what happens in an eclipse . . . . where
and what is the Equator and why is it hot there?
If you turn to page 20 you will find some questions on the
poems themselves and some more things to do.

15

Sunning

Old Dog lay in the summer sun
Much too lazy to rise and run.
He flapped an ear
At a buzzing fly;
He winked a half-opened
Sleepy eye;
He scratched himself
On an itching spot;
As he dozed on the porch
When the sun was hot.
He whimpered a bit
From force of habit,
While he lazily dreamed
Of chasing a rabbit.
But Old Dog happily lay in the sun,
Much too lazy to rise and run.

JAMES S. TIPPETT

A Hot Day

Cottonwool clouds loiter.
A lawnmower, very far,
Birrs. Then a bee comes
To a crimson rose and softly,
Deftly and fatly crams
A velvet body in.

A tree, June-lazy, makes
A tent of dim green light.
Sunlight weaves in the leaves,
Honey-light laced with leaf-light,
Green interleaved with gold.

Sunlight gathers its rays
In sheaves, which the wind unweaves
And then reweaves — the wind
That puffs a smell of grass
Through the heat-heavy, trembling
Summer pool of air.

A.S.J. TESSIMOND

A Dragonfly

When the heat of the summer
Made drowsy the land,
A dragonfly came
And sat on my hand,

With its blue jointed body,
And wings like spun glass,
It lit on my fingers
As though they were grass.

ELEANOR FARJEON

In June

In June, haymaking, and heavy bees
Suddenly swarming on sagging branches;
Swifts dart, wheel about the hot sky,
Glide over pools, green with weed and dragonflies.
Sheep, streaming down from the hills to be shorn,
Cry all night to the thin wind;
Corn turns copper and gold in long fields, moon
   daisies,
Whiter than midnight moths, tower over pimpernels,
Waiting to close red eyes at sundown;
Rain falls in a kind shower.
In June, all days are cherry ripe,
Sweeter than strawberries.

LEONARD CLARK

July Night

July night, every pond
Standing green, deep in weed and moonlight.
Newts are baby dragons, fast asleep
Beneath the muddy stones, and toads
Have emerald eyes.
All streams run soft with miller's thumbs,
Dace and floating stars,
The silver minnows are at peace.
And now a nervous shrew comes out
To drink his midnight fill,
An owl glides by on hunting wing,
The grasses sip the dangling dew.
Over the hill the first shrill cock prepares
To bugle in the day;
And heavy cows will soon be streaming in
From misty fields, and down the ferny lane
A farm gate creaks.

LEONARD CLARK

from **July**

Loud is the summer's busy song;
The smallest breeze can find a tongue;
While insects of each tiny size
Grow teasing with their melodies,
Till noon burns with its blistering breath
Around, and day dies still as death.
The busy noise of man and brute
Is on a sudden lost and mute;
Even the brook that leaps along
Seems weary of its bubbling song,
And, so soft its waters creep,
Tired silence sinks in sounder sleep.

JOHN CLARE

August

The city dwellers all complain
When August comes and brings no rain.
The pavements burn upon their feet;
Temper and temperature compete.
They mop their brows, they slow their pace,
And wish they were some other place.

But farmers do not mind the heat;
They know it ripens corn and wheat.
They love to see the sun rise red,
Remembering what their fathers said:
'An August month that's dry and warm
Will never do the harvest harm.'

MICHAEL LEWIS

In August

A snake coiled on a hot white stone,
  A bright fish in a pool,
A huge sun burning in the sky
  And holidays from school.

Where willow trees admire themselves
  In the pool's looking-glass,
Rippling on air the electric hum
  Of insects shakes the grass.

And in this world of August
  One solitary boy
Finds in a single day of bliss
  Eternities of joy.

JOHN SMITH

Poetry Close-up

1. Look at the poem called 'A Hot Day'. It is about a very sunny day, so why does it say that the light is 'dim'?

2. Look at Eleanor Farjeon's poem 'A Dragonfly'. Why do you think she says that the dragonfly had 'wings like spun glass'?

3. Now look at the two poems written by Leonard Clark.
   a) In the poem 'In June', why does he describe rain as 'kind'?
   b) Why do you think he describes newts as 'baby dragons' in 'July Night'?
   c) What are the 'miller's thumbs' mentioned in the poem 'July Night'?
   d) In both the poems he uses the word 'heavy' — once to describe bees and once to describe cows. What is making each of them heavy?

4. Read the poem called 'August' by Michael Lewis. Describe the different attitudes of the city dwellers and the farmers to the weather.

5. Write a story in which you imagine there has been no rain for several months.

Other Things To Do

.... Can you find out how heat affects different things, for example, metals and liquids .... what happens to air when it gets hot?

.... Why do people perspire or sweat? .... discover how different animals keep cool.

.... How does temperature affect warm-blooded and cold-blooded animals?

.... How does a hot-air balloon work?

Autumn

"The rustle of leaves
A chill in the air"

In this section you will find some poets'
thoughts on autumn. Read the poems and think
about these questions on this season of change.

What happens to living things in autumn?

.... Think of — golden leaves .... rosy apples ....
falling seeds .... scurrying animals
.... migrating birds.

What is different about the weather?

.... Think of — sudden changes .... rolling mist ....
patchy fog .... damp earth .... shorter
days and longer nights.

If you wish to write your own poem, these words may help you.

crisp	musty	wood smoke	spiral	flutter	spin
dull	crimson	scarlet	evergreen	glide	float
bronze	hazy	russet	scuffle	whirl	swirl
mellow	chestnuts	rustle	crunch	twirl	

Autumn Action

Animal activity changes in autumn. Here are four
British wild animals: fox; badger; squirrel;
hedgehog.
Choose one of them and make a detailed study of
it .... draw a sketch of the animal .... how does it
prepare for the winter? .... what does it eat? ....
find out the name of its home and describe it.
Autumn is a time when trees spread their seeds.
Can you find out four different ways in which this
happens?
If you turn to page 27 you will find some questions
on the poems themselves and some more things
to do.

Autumn

Yellow the bracken,
Golden the sheaves,
Rosy the apples,
Crimson the leaves;
Mist on the hillside,
Clouds grey and white.
Autumn, good morning!
Summer, good night.

FLORENCE HOATSON

August Ends

A nip in the air today, and autumn
Playing hide and seek with summer;
Winter takes a first grip on plant, insect, bird.
Last blackberry flowers fade,
And fruit, moving from green to red,
Dangles foot long purple clusters
Over downy hedgerows, wasps go numb,
Fall drowsy on dropped plums, honey and smokey wax
Perfume the spidered loft, barley shines.
Swifts on curved wings wheel overhead
Printing broad arrows on the leaden sky;
And now I catch the echo of the far north wind
And over the shorn and stubbled land
The dreaded hawk hovers, and a cloud of peewits cry.

LEONARD CLARK

22

Something Told the Wild Geese

Something told the wild geese
   It was time to go.
Though the fields lay golden
   Something whispered—'Snow'.
Leaves were green and stirring,
   Berries, lustre-glossed,
But beneath warm feathers
   Something cautioned—'Frost'.

All the sagging orchards
   Steamed with amber spice,
But each wild breast stiffened
   At remembered ice.
Something told the wild geese
   It was time to fly—
Summer sun was on their wings,
   Winter in their cry.

RACHEL FIELD

Sweet Chestnuts

How still the woods were! Not a redbreast whistled
To mark the end of a mild autumn day.
Under the trees the chestnut-cases lay,
Looking like small green hedgehogs softly bristled.

Plumply they lay, each with its fruit packed tight;
For when we rolled them gently with our feet,
The outer shells burst wide apart and split,
Showing the chestnuts brown and creamy-white.

Quickly we kindled a bright fire of wood,
And placed them in the ashes. There we sat,
Listening how all our chestnuts popped and spat.
And then, the smell how rich, the taste how good!

JOHN WALSH

from **The One Singer**

Dead leaves from off the tree
Make whirlpools on the ground;
Like dogs that chase their tails,
Those leaves go round and round;
Like birds unfledged and young,
The old bare branches cry;
Branches that shake and bend
To feel the winds go by.

W.H. DAVIES

Leaves and Fires

They are raking the leaves in the parks of the town,
They are dying, the leaves, they are all falling down,
Twirling and whirling, the leaves die away,
Falling all night, raking all day.

They are stoking the fires in the parks of the town,
They are smoking, the fires, they are all burning brown,
Sweeping and piling, the fires are alight,
Burning all day, smoking all night.

LEONARD CLARK

Colour

The world is full of colour!
  'Tis Autumn once again
And leaves of gold and crimson
  Are lying in the lane.

There are brown and yellow acorns,
  Berries and scarlet haws,
Amber gorse and heather
  Purple across the moors!

Green apples in the orchard,
  Flushed by a glowing sun;
Mellow pears and brambles
  Where coloured pheasants run!

Yellow, blue and orange,
  Russet, rose and red—
A gaily-coloured pageant—
  An Autumn flower bed.

Beauty of light and shadow,
  Glory of wheat and rye,
Colour of shining water
  Under a sunset sky!

ADELINE WHITE

Seeds

Seeds that twist and seeds that twirl,
Seeds with wings which spin and whirl;

Seeds that float on thistledown,
Seeds in coats of glossy brown;

Seeds that burst with popping sound
From their pods to reach the ground;

Seeds with hooks that clutch and cling;
Seeds I plant for flowers next spring;

Seeds of every shape and size,
Soon will sleep 'neath winter skies.

HILDA I. ROSTRON

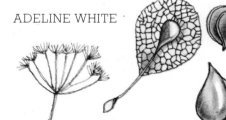

Leaf-fall

Golden, yellow, brown and red,
Pirouetting overhead.
See them flutter, twist and curl
Dancing in a windblown whirl.
Till upon the ground they lie
With a brittle dying sigh,
Buried in the earth's warm bed,
Wrapped in coats of brown and red.

E.H. RAY

25

Autumn

A touch of cold in the Autumn night—
I walked abroad,
And saw the ruddy moon lean over a hedge
Like a red-faced farmer.
I did not stop to speak, but nodded,
And round about were the wistful stars
With white faces like town children.

T.E. HULME

November

No sun — no moon!
No morn — no noon!
No dawn — no dusk — no proper time of day —
No sky — no earthly view —
No distance looking blue —
No road — no street — no 't'other side the way' —
No end to any Row —
No indications where the Crescents go —
No top to any steeple —
No recognitions of familiar people —
No courtesies for showing 'em —
No knowing 'em!
No mail — no post —
No news from any foreign coast —
No park — no ring — no afternoon gentility —
No company — no nobility —
No warmth, no cheerfulness, no healthful ease,
No comfortable feel in any member —
No shade, no shine, no butterflies, no bees,
No fruits, no flowers, no leaves, no birds,
November!

THOMAS HOOD

Poetry Close-up

1. In the poem 'August Ends' Leonard Clark says
    'and autumn
    Playing hide and seek with summer'.
    Why does he say that?

2. Look at the poem 'Something Told the Wild
    Geese'. How do the geese know that it is time to
    go and where are they going?

3. Adeline White, in her poem 'Colour', tells us that
    the leaves are like a 'pageant'. Why do you think
    she uses that word?

4. In the poem 'Leaf-fall', what is meant by
    pirouetting?

5. How many different words can you find from the
    poems which describe:
    . . . . the colour of the leaves;
    . . . . the movement of the seeds and leaves?

6. Imagine a conversation between a tree which is
    losing its leaves and an evergreen. Write down
    what you think they might say.

Other Things To Do

. . . . Make a Class Autumn Interest Table.

. . . . Create an autumn collage using leaves, leaf
prints, seeds, bark, etc.

. . . . Write about and draw a common evergreen tree.
Do the same for one which loses its leaves in
autumn. What do you call this type of tree?

. . . . Listen to Vivaldi's 'The Four Seasons'.

Winter

"Winter is the king of showmen
Turning tree stumps into snowmen"

In this section you will find some poets'
thoughts on how winter affects people and the
landscape. Read the poems and think about these
questions on our coldest season.

How would you describe winter weather?

.... Think of — frozen ground .... icy water ....
frosted windows .... swirling
snowflakes .... a silent world.

What does winter mean to you?

.... Think of — throwing snowballs .... building
snowmen .... making slides.

.... Think of — skidding wheels .... shivering people
.... dangerous ice .... stranded farms.

If you wish to write your own poem, these words may help you.

sparkle	flurry	bitter	brittle	icicles	crystals	settle
crisp	raw	biting	chill	harsh	slush	treacherous
tingle	bleak	chatter	float	melt	thaw	ruddy

Winter Worlds

Use an atlas or globe to find the North and South
Poles.

Scott, Admunsen and Shackleton were
leaders of three Polar Expeditions.
.... Where did they come from? .... draw a
map of their routes .... how did they
travel? .... what difficulties did they
face?

If you turn to page 34 you will find some questions on
the poems themselves and some more things to do.

Snow

This morning
 as I lay in bed
I wondered how
 the sky had shed
its darkness
 and had left around
a million snowflakes
 on the ground.
The air was strange
 and still, and light:
it wasn't either
 day or night.
Although the moon
 had gone away
it wasn't either
 night or day —
but curious
 and magical
as if it were
 no time at all . . . .
The trees were waiting.
 Every house
was still and silent,
 Not a mouse
stirred
 in that silken land.
I know
 it was enchanted
by the snow.

JEAN KENWARD

Frozen Stiff

Stiff as a battleship
prim as a pin
look at the washing
the frost is in!

Nighties, pyjamas
and petticoats too—
hard as the button
upon my shoe;

Punch them and pull them
they won't let go
of the long clothes line
for they love it so;

And however you tug them
they hold on tight
to the shivering pegs
with all their might,

As if they would cry
"Oh, leave us, please!
We love to hang here
and freeze and freeze!"

Look at my trousers,
there's ice on the hem!
I shan't sit down
when I'm wearing them!

JEAN KENWARD

Winter Morning

Winter is the king of showmen,
Turning tree stumps into snowmen
And houses into birthday cakes
And spreading sugar over the lakes.
Smooth and clean and frost white
The world looks good enough to bite.
That's the season to be young,
Catching snowflakes on your tongue.

Snow is snowy when it's snowing
I'm sorry it's slushy when it's going.

OGDEN NASH

The Snowflake

Before I melt,
Come, look at me!
This lovely icy filigree!
Of a great forest
In one night
I make a wilderness
Of white:
By skyey cold
Of crystal made,
All softly, on
Your finger laid,
I pause, that you
My beauty see:
Breathe, and I vanish
Instantly.

WALTER DE LA MARE

Snow

No breath of wind,
No gleam of sun —
Still the white snow
Whirls softly down —
Twig and bough
And blade and thorn
All in an icy
Quiet, forlorn.

Whispering, rustling,
Through the air,
On sill and stone,
Roof — everywhere,
It heaps its powdery
Crystal flakes:
Of every tree
A mountain makes;
Till pale and faint
At shut of day,
Stoops from the West
One wintry ray.
And, feathered in fire,
Where ghosts the moon,
A robin shrills
His lonely tune.

WALTER DE LA MARE

from **Snow in the Suburbs**

Every branch big with it,
Bent every twig with it;
Every fork like a white web-foot;
Every street and pavement mute:
Some flakes have lost their way, and grope back
    upward, when
Meeting those meandering down they turn and
    descend again.
The palings are glued together like a wall,
And there is no waft of wind with the fleecy fall.

THOMAS HARDY

Frost

The January morning dawned cold and misty grey,
But on the trees, and lawn, and hedge
The powdered hoar frost lay.
Lace cobwebs from the rambling rose
Hung delicate and white;
Jack Frost had worked his magic
In the silent, star-filled night,
So the garden should be beautiful,
Not dull, it should be bright,
And every twig and web ablaze
With tinselled strings of light.
Wake up, shine out in splendour,
You round, red morning sun,
Shine out and make a fairyland
Before the frost has gone.

LILLIAN BOUCHER

White Fields

In the winter time we go
Walking in the fields of snow;

Where there is no grass at all;
Where the top of every wall,

Every fence, and every tree
Is as white as white can be.

Pointing out the way we came —
Every one of them the same —

All across the fields there be
Prints in silver filligree;

And our mothers always know,
By the footprints in the snow,

Where it is the children go.

JAMES STEPHENS

Death of a Snowman

I was awake all night,
Big as a polar bear,
Strong and firm and white.
The tall black hat I wear
Was draped with ermine fur.
I felt so fit and well
Till the world began to stir.
And the morning sun swell.
I was tired, began to yawn;
At noon in the humming sun
I caught a severe warm;
My nose began to run.
My hat grew black and fell,
Was followed by my grey head.
There was no funeral bell,
But by tea-time I was dead.

VERNON SCANNELL

from **London Snow**   **Winter Days**

When men were all asleep the snow came flying,
In large white flakes falling on the city brown,
Stealthily and perpetually settling and loosely lying,
    Hushing the latest traffic of the drowsy town;
Deadening, muffling, stifling its murmurs failing;
Lazily and incessantly floating down and down;
    Silently sifting and veiling road, roof and railing;
Hiding difference, making unevenness even,
Into angles and crevices softly drifting and sailing.

ROBERT BRIDGES

Biting air
Winds blow
City streets
Under snow

Noses red
Lips sore
Runny eyes
Hands raw

Chimneys smoke
Cars crawl
Piled snow
On garden wall

Slush in gutters
Ice in lanes
Frosty patterns
On window panes

Morning call
Lift up head
Nipped by winter
Stay in bed

GARETH OWEN

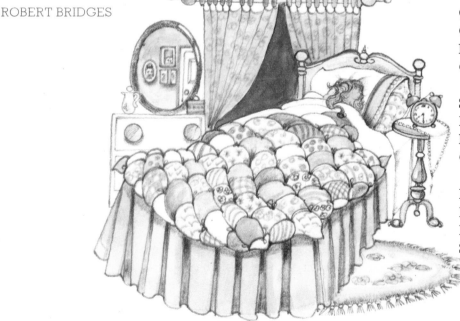

33

Poetry Close-up

1. In the poem 'Frozen Stiff' by Jean Kenward, what has made the washing as stiff as a battleship?

2. In the poem 'Winter Morning' by Ogden Nash, how are tree stumps turned into snowmen and houses into birthday cakes?

3. Walter de la Mare says in his poem 'Snow' that 'of every tree a mountain makes'. Do you think that snow *would* make every tree look like a mountain, or is he describing one special type of tree?

4. In the poem 'London Snow', what phrase does Robert Bridges use to show that the snow makes everything smooth?

5. Find as many words and phrases as you can from the poems which describe how snow makes the world silent.

6. Write a story called 'Lost in a Blizzard'.

Other Things To Do

.... What is hypothermia? Find out about who it is most likely to affect.

.... How are snow and ice formed?

.... Look at snowflakes under a microscope. Can you draw them?

.... Find out why pipes burst in winter.

.... Draw and write about Eskimos.

.... Find out about the Ice Ages .... when did they occur? .... what sort of creatures lived during these times?

The Weather

Whatever the Weather

Whether the weather be fine
Or whether the weather be not,
Whether the weather be cold
Or whether the weather be hot,
We'll weather the weather
Whatever the weather,
Whether we like it or not.

ANON.

A Wet Day

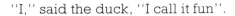

"I," said the duck, "I call it fun".

Is this your idea of a rainy day? Now think about these questions which might help you to write down your own thoughts.

What happens on rainy days?

.... Think of — wet playtimes .... steamed up windows .... playing in puddles.

.... Think of — dashing for shelter .... dripping umbrellas .... soggy clothes.

Do storms frighten you?

.... Think of— flooded homes .... rumbling thunder .... flashing lightning .... raging torrents.

If you wish to write your own poem, these words may help you.

dismal	violent	vivid	fork	trickle
squelch	deluge	gentle	piercing	saturate
splash	drizzle	torrential	rainbow	leaden
gush	soak	glisten	downpour	refresh

Water's Ways

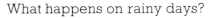

Canals are one way in which man has used water for transport.
Can you find out which was the first widely used canal in Britain? .... draw a map of its route?

Can you find information about these ....
navvies .... towpaths .... leggers .... butty boats .... canal people .... locks .... aqueducts?

What can you find out about these famous international waterways? .... Suez Canal .... Panama Canal .... St. Lawrence Seaway.

If you turn to page 43 you will find some questions on the poems themselves and some more things to do.

Rain

There are holes in the sky
Where the rain gets in,
But they're ever so small
That's why rain is thin.

SPIKE MILLIGAN

Who Likes the Rain?

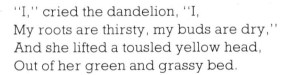

"I," said the duck, "I call it fun,
For I have my pretty red rubbers on;
They make a little three-toed track
In the soft, cool mud—quack! quack!"

"I," cried the dandelion, "I,
My roots are thirsty, my buds are dry,"
And she lifted a tousled yellow head,
Out of her green and grassy bed.

Sang the brook, "I welcome every drop,
Come down, dear raindrops; never stop
Until a broad river you make of me,
And then I will carry you to the sea."

"I," shouted Ted, "for I can run,
With my high-top boots and raincoat on,
Through every puddle and runlet and pool
I find on the road to school."

ANON.

from **Rain in Summer**

How beautiful is the rain!
After the dust and heat,
In the broad and fiery street,
In the narrow lane,
How beautiful is the rain!

How it clatters along the roofs,
Like the tramp of hoofs!
How it gushes and struggles out
From the throat of the overflowing spout!

Across the window-pane
It pours and pours;
And swift and wide,
With a muddy tide,
Like a river down the gutter roars
The rain, the welcome rain.

HENRY WADSWORTH LONGFELLOW

A Rainy Day

The sky is grey today,
The birds swoop low.
The trees are black as night,
A robin hops along the wet wall top,
His breast is the brightest thing on this dull day.
Water drips from the trees,
Raindrops are like jewels on the grass,
The path shines like a stream,
But soon the clouds will float away.
The sun will shine more brightly after rain,
The birds will flap their wings for joy,
The jewels will dissolve in the grass,
And I will ride my bike again.

ANDREW WEST

Rainy Nights

I like the town on rainy nights
When everything is wet—
When all the town has magic lights
And streets of shining jet!

When all the rain about the town
Is like a looking-glass,
And all the lights are upside down
Below me as I pass.

In all the pools are velvet skies,
And down the dazzling street
A fairy city gleams and lies
In beauty at my feet.

IRENE THOMPSON

Rain

The lights are all on, though it's just past midday,
There are no more indoor games we can play,
No one can think of anything to say,
It rained all yesterday, it's raining today,
It's grey outside, inside me it's grey.

I stare out of the window, fist under my chin,
The gutter leaks drips on the lid of the dustbin,
When they say 'Cheer up', I manage a grin,
I draw a fish on the glass with a sail-sized fin,
It's sodden outside, and it's damp within.

Matches, bubbles and papers pour into the drains,
Clouds smother the sad laments from the trains,
Grandad says it brings on his rheumatic pains,
The moisture's got right inside of my brains,
It's raining outside, inside me it rains.

BRIAN LEE

from **Summer Storm**

Look! look! that livid flash!
And instantly follows the rattling thunder,
As if some cloud-crag, split asunder,
Fell, splintering with a ruinous crash
On the earth, which crouches in silence under;
And now a solid grey of rain
Shuts off the landscape, mile by mile.

JAMES RUSSELL LOWELL

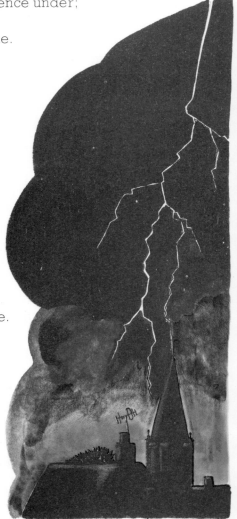

Thunder and Lightning

Blood punches through every vein
As lightning strips the window pane.

Under its flashing whip, a white
Village leaps to light.

On tubs of thunder, fists of rain
Slog it out of sight again.

Blood punches the heart with fright
As rain belts the village night.

JAMES KIRKUP

Storm

Bursting on the suburbs with dynamic gusts of energy
And concentrated fury comes the mad March gale.
Blowing off the roofing-felt, which lies atop the
    garden-sheds,
Encountering the window with a splash of sleet and
    hail.
Distending all the trousers on the wildly waving
    washing-line,
Drumming on the window like a hanged man's heels,
Swaying all the aitches of the television aerials,
Muddying the roadway, 'neath the slowly turning
    wheels.
Gentlemen in overcoats pursuing trilbies hopelessly
Cursing at the vigour of the brusque March gale,
And lightning lights the darkening sky with bright
    celestial clarity,
While women in their kitchens hear the thunder and
    turn pale.
Ear-lobes reddening at the slashing of the hail-stones,
Nose-tips deadening at the coldness of the sleet,
Eye-lids wincing at the brightness of the lightning
Wet stones glistening beneath the hurried feet.
White marbles bouncing on the flat roofs of the
    garages,
Black sky paling as the storm dies down,
Wet folk emerging from the haven of a doorway
As the sun comes out again and smiles upon the town.

R.N. BARTLETT

In the Rain

There is no colour in the rain
It's only water, wet and plain.
It makes damp spots upon my book
And splashes on my new dress, look!
But puddles, in the rainy weather,
Glisten like a peacock's feather.

RENÉ CLOKE

Mrs. Golightly

Mrs. Golightly's goloshes
   Are roomy and large;
Through water she slithers and sloshes,
   As safe as a barge.

When others at home must be stopping,
   To market she goes,
And returns later on with her shopping
   Tucked into her toes.

JAMES REEVES

Poetry Close-up

1. In the poem 'Rain in Summer', which animal is compared to the rain and why?

2. In the poem 'A Rainy Day' by Andrew West, explain why the path shines.

3. In the poem 'Rain' by Brian Lee, which phrase in the second verse shows that the poet feels miserable?

4. Why does the poet describe lightning as 'livid' in the poem 'Summer Storm'?

5. Look at the poem 'Storm' by R.N. Bartlett. Can you explain these phrases?
   'Distending all the trousers'
   'White marbles'.

6. In the poem 'In the Rain' by René Cloke, why do the puddles glisten 'like a peacock's feather'?

7. Look at the poem 'Mrs. Golightly'. Find out what goloshes are.

8. Find all the words used in the poems which describe the sound of the rain.

9. Write a story called — 'When the Rain Wouldn't Stop'.

Other Things To Do

. . . . What does a meteorologist do?

. . . . Look at a rainfall map of your country. Which places have most rainfall?

. . . . Find out about the Great Flood mentioned in the Old Testament.

. . . . If you can, try different instruments to make up your own music about rain. Record your music when you have finished.

A Windy Day

"Who has seen the wind?"

This is a question asked by one poet. Of course no one really sees the wind. We only see its effects. Here are some more questions to help you describe this invisible force.

How does the wind affect us?

.... Think of — scattered paper .... swirling dust .... billowing clothes .... umbrellas turned inside out .... swaying trees .... broken branches .... flying slates.

What sounds do you hear on a windy day?

.... Think of — rustling leaves .... rolling milk bottles .... slamming doors .... rattling windows .... telephone wires whistling.

If you wish to write your own poem, these words may help you.

whine	flap	lash	blustery	wail	whirl
moan	flutter	whip	murmur	creak	tear
howl	scurry	screech	sigh	crash	clang
shriek	groan	gust	whisper	bend	clatter

Winds and Waves

Hundreds of years ago, nearly all ships were powered by wind. A sailor's life then was very different to that of today.

.... Write about and draw the following: press gangs .... cat-o'-nine-tails .... walking the plank .... scurvy .... cannons .... cutlasses .... sea shanties .... uniforms .... the crow's-nest.

.... Find out all you can about these famous sailors: Drake .... Magellan .... Cook .... Blackbeard.

If you turn to page 49 you will find some questions on the poems themselves and some more things to do.

Granny

Through every nook and every cranny
The wind blew in on poor old Granny;
Around her knees, into each ear
(And up her nose as well, I fear).

All through the night the wind grew worse,
It nearly made the vicar curse.
The top had fallen off the steeple
Just missing him (and other people).

It blew on man; it blew on beast.
It blew on nun; it blew on priest.
It blew the wig off Auntie Fanny —
But most of all, it blew on Granny!

SPIKE MILLIGAN

Wind Song

When the wind blows
The quiet things speak.
Some whisper, some clang,
Some creak.

Grasses swish.
Treetops sigh.
Flags slap
and snap at the sky.
Wires on poles
whistle and hum.
Ashcans roll.
Windows drum.

The Wind

I can get through a doorway without any key,
And strip the leaves from the great oak tree.

I can drive storm-clouds and shake tall towers,
Or steal through a garden and not wake the flowers.

Seas I can move and ships I can sink;
I can carry a house-top or the scent of a pink.

When I am angry I can rave and riot;
And when I am spent, I lie quiet as quiet.

JAMES REEVES

When the wind goes—
suddenly
then,
the quiet things
are quiet again.

LILIAN MOORE

THE POETRY LIBRARY

The Wind

Who has seen the wind?
　　Neither I nor you;
But when the leaves hang trembling
　　The wind is passing through.

Who has seen the wind?
　　Neither you nor I;
But when the trees bow down their heads
　　The wind is passing by.

CHRISTINA ROSSETTI

A Windy Day

The wind brings all dead things to life,
Branches that lash the air like whips
And dead leaves rolling in a hurry
Or peering in a rabbit's bury
Or trying to push down a tree;
Gates that fly open to the wind
And close again behind,
And fields that are a flowing sea
And make the cattle look like ships;
Straws glistening and stiff
Lying on air as on a shelf
And pond that leaps to leave itself;
And feathers too that rise and float,
Each feather changed into a bird,
And line-hung sheets that crack and strain;
Even the sun-greened coat,
That through so many winds has served,
The scarecrow struggles to put on again.

ANDREW YOUNG

The Wind

The wind is a wolf
That sniffs at doors
And rattles windows
With his paws.

Hidden in the night,
He rushes round
The locked-up house
Making angry sounds.

He leaps on the roof
And tries to drive
Away the house
And everything inside.

Tired next morning,
The wind's still there
Snatching pieces of paper
And ruffling your hair.

He quietens down and in the end
You hardly notice him go
Whispering down the road
To find another place to blow.

STANLEY COOK

46

from **A Song of Wind**

Hark to the song of the scattering, scurrying,
Blustering, bullying, bellowing, hurrying
    Wind!
Over the hills it comes, laughing and rollicking,
Curling and whirling, flying and frolicking,
   Spinning the clouds that are scattered and thinned.
     And shouting a song
     As it gallops along—
  A song that is nothing but wind.

This is the song of the galloping, hurrying,
Gusty, and dusty, and whirling, and worrying
    Wind.
Over the hills it comes laughing and rollicking,
Yelling, and swooping, and flying, and frolicking,
   Shaking the fences so solidly pinned,
     And shrieking a song
     As it gallops along—
  A terrible song that is wind.

WILL LAWSON

Gale Warning

The wind breaks bound, tossing the oak and chestnut,
Whirling the paper at street corners,
The city clerks are harassed, wrestling head-down:
The gulls are blown inland.

Three slates fall from a roof,
The promenade is in danger:
Inland, the summer fête is postponed,
The British glider record broken.

The wind blows through the city, cleansing,
Whipping the posters from the hoardings,
Tearing the bunting and the banners,
The wind blows steadily, and as it will.

MICHAEL ROBERTS

Poetry Close-up

1. What do you think Granny feels about the wind in the poem by Spike Milligan?

2. In the poem 'Granny', what is meant by a 'nook'?

3. In the poem 'A Windy Day' give an example of how a dead thing is brought to life.

4. From the poem 'The Wind' by Stanley Cook, write out two different lines which describe a gentle breeze and a strong wind.

5. The last line of 'A Song of Wind' by Will Lawson describes the wind as 'a terrible song'. Why does the poet also say it 'comes laughing'?

6. In the poem 'Gale Warning' by Michael Roberts, why is the promenade in danger?

7. List all the words used in the poems to describe the sound of the wind.

8. Imagine you are blown by the wind to a strange land. Describe your journey and other adventures.

Other Things To Do

.... Find out about winds —

What causes them?
What is the Beaufort Scale?
Gales are very strong winds. In some parts of the world they have different names, for example, whirlwind, hurricane, typhoon, cyclone, tornado, sirocco. Find out as much as you can about them.

A Foggy Day

"The fog comes
on little cat feet."

The writer of these lines sees fog as creeping up on us. Read the poems and see what other writers have to say. Then think about these questions on fog.

What is it like to be out on a foggy day?

.... Think of — sinister shapes .... muffled footsteps .... eerie silence .... mysterious sounds .... looming buildings .... swirling patches .... dimmed lights .... a world of grey.

Can fog be dangerous?

.... Think of — crashing cars .... people lost .... collisions at sea .... wailing fog-horns.

If you wish to write your own poem, these words may help you.

dense	ghostly	clammy	dank	swirl	envelop
thick	cloaked	choking	damp	hang	seep
opaque	blanket	ominous	cough	veiled	chilly

Foggy Focus

When we go out in the fog, it makes us understand the importance of our eyes. Some people have eyesight problems. How are they helped?

.... Write about Louis Braille and his alphabet.
.... Describe how guide dogs are trained.
.... Give two reasons why some people need to wear glasses.
.... Explain what colour blindness means.

If you turn to page 54 you will find some questions on the poems themselves and some more things to do.

Fog

The fog comes
on little cat feet.
It sits looking
over harbour and city
on silent haunches
and then moves on.

CARL SANDBURG

Mist

Subtle as an illusionist
The deft hands of the morning mist
Play tricks upon my sight:
Haystacks dissolve and hedges lift
Out of the unseen fields and drift
Between the veils of white.

On the horizon, heads of trees
Swim with the mist about their knees,
And when the farm dogs bark,
I turn to watch how on the calm
Of that white sea, the red-roofed farm
Floats like a Noah's Ark.

DOUGLAS GIBSON

Fog in November

Fog in November, trees have no heads,
Streams only sound, walls suddenly stop
Half-way up hills, the ghost of a man spreads
Dung on dead fields for next year's crop.
I cannot see my hand before my face,
My body does not seem to be my own,
The world becomes a far-off, foreign place,
People are strangers, houses silent, unknown.

LEONARD CLARK

The Fog

I saw the fog grow thick,
Which soon made blind my ken;
It made tall men of boys,
And giants of tall men.

It clutched my throat, I coughed;
Nothing was in my head
Except two heavy eyes
Like balls of burning lead.

And when it grew so black
That I could know no place,
I lost all judgement then,
Of distance and of space.

The street lamps, and the lights
Upon the halted cars,
Could either be the earth
Or be the heavenly stars.

A man passed by me close,
I asked my way; he said
'Come, follow me, my friend' —
I followed where he led.

He rapped the stones in front,
'Trust me,' he said 'and come.'
I followed like a child —
A blind man led me home.

W.H. DAVIES

The Fog

Slowly, the fog,
Hunch-shouldered with a grey face,
Arms wide, advances,
Finger-tips touching the way
Past the dark houses
And dark gardens of roses.
Up the short street from the harbour,
Slowly the fog,
Seeking, seeking;
Arms wide, shoulders hunched,
Searching, searching.
Out through the streets to the fields,
Slowly, the fog—
A blind man hunting the moon.

F.R. McCREARY

November Mist

Curling and swirling, silent and soft,
Into the cellar and into the loft,
Creeping through keyholes and under the door,
The mists of November are with us once more.

They're cold and they're damp, but they're beautiful
    too,
And the view from the window seems magic and new,
For the mist's pearl-grey gown each house does
    enfold
And gives to each street-lamp a halo of gold.

BERNARD W. MARTIN

Poetry Close-up

1. Why do you think Carl Sandburg compares the fog with a cat?

2. Douglas Gibson, in his poem 'Mist', uses the word 'illusionist'. Can you find out what this means?

3. Why does Leonard Clark, in his poem 'Fog in November', say that 'trees have no heads'?

4. Which part of the day do you think F.R. McCreary is writing about in his poem 'The Fog'?

5. Find four words from the poems which describe the colour of the fog.

6. The movement of the fog is described in many of the poems. Can you list some of the words and phrases which do this?

7. Read the poem 'The Fog' by W.H. Davies. It tells us a story. Write this story in your own words.

Other Things To Do

. . . . Discover what causes fog.

. . . . Find out about the difference between fog and smog. Write about smokeless zones and air pollution.

. . . . We use many things to help us overcome the dangers of fog. Find out about lighthouses . . . . fog-horns . . . . radar . . . . cat's eyes . . . . automatic pilots on aircraft.

Special Days and Festivals

The Hippopotamus's Birthday

He has opened all his parcels
  but the largest and the last;
His hopes are at their highest
  and his heart is beating fast.
O happy Hippopotamus,
  what lovely gift is here?
He cuts the string. The world stands still.
  A pair of boots appear!

O little Hippopotamus,
  the sorrows of the small!
He dropped two tears to mingle
  with the flowing Senegal;
And the 'Thank you' that he uttered
  was the saddest ever heard
In the Senegambian jungle
  from the mouth of beast or bird.

E.V. RIEU

Harvest

"Festival of food as summer fades"

In this section you will find some poems about harvest time. Read the poems and then think about these questions.

What is collected at harvest time?

.... Think of — golden corn .... rosy apples .... juicy pears .... ripe blackberries.

What was the harvest like many years ago?

.... Think of — slashing scythes .... straining horses .... creaking carts .... weary workers.

What is different about a modern harvest?

.... Think of — clattering machines .... combine harvesters .... produce on the move .... packing, canning, freezing .... supermarket shelves.

If you wish to write your own poem, these words may help you.

plough	throb	ears	grow	heavy	gather
ripen	growl	mellow	reap	abundant	pluck
yellow	diesel	fruits	swollen	packed	tractor
laden	roar	grain	sway	windmills	rumbling

Harvest Highlights

Many of our foods and drinks come from abroad. These include sugar from the West Indies, rice from China, coffee from Brazil, and tea from Sri Lanka. Choose one of them .... draw the plant it comes from and describe it .... write about how it is grown and harvested .... the processes it undergoes before we use it .... draw a map showing other countries where this crop is grown.

If you turn to page 60 you will find some questions on the poems themselves and some more things to do.

The Harvest

The silver rain, the shining sun,
The fields where scarlet poppies run,
And all the ripples of the wheat
Are in the bread that I do eat.

So when I sit for every meal
And say a grace, I always feel
That I am eating rain and sun,
And fields where scarlet poppies run.

ALICE C. HENDERSON

Corn and Nuts

Corn harvest nearly done, and silver wheat
Is packed away in barns and bags,
The barley wears a gold beard still,
But poppies are dressed up in rags.
The fields look bare, and finches meet
In greedy flocks like scavengers,
Pecking the stubble stalks, and eat their fill;
And overhead a partridge whirrs.

Nut harvest then, and boys in noisy gangs
Invade the quiet of the glades,
And with long sticks pull down the brown-shelled
   crop,
Each cluster, that on sagging branches hangs
Over the mossy floor where bracken fades
And, black with fruit, the tangled brambles bend;
The squirrel retreats, the boys move off, and stop
To share their spoils beyond the dark wood's end.

And so do corn and nuts have their increase,
Their harvest come, the fields and woods at peace.

LEONARD CLARK

Harvests

For one more day and windless night
The fields stand gold, and poppies burn
At peace among the lines of straw;
And then the reapers come.

The proud corn falls, and breathless mice
Run terrified with rats and voles
To find a refuge in the hedge;
And then the weasels come.

LEONARD CLARK

Harvest Home

The wagons loom like blue caravans in the dusk:
They lumber mysteriously down the moonlight lanes.

We ride on the stacks of rust gold corn,
Filling the sky with our song.

The horses toss their heads and the harness-bells
Jingle all the way.

HERBERT READ

August Weather

Dead heat and windless air,
    And silence over all;
Never a leaf astir,
    But the ripe apples fall;
Plums are purple-red,
    Pears amber and brown;
Thud! in the garden-bed!
    Ripe apples fall down.

Air like a cider-press
    With the bruised apples' scent;
Low whistles express
    Some sleepy bird's content;
Still world and windless sky,
    A mist of heat o'er all;
Peace like a lullaby,
    And the ripe apples fall.

KATHARINE TYNAN

Windmill Jack

High on the hill
stands Windmill Jack:
He's got four sails
upon his back,
and when the wind is up
I know
round and round
his four sails go;

Round and round
and round again
they trundle and they turn
and then —
CREAK AND CRUNKLE
CREAK AND CRACK —
"Hark at me!"
says Windmill Jack.

"All the time
my sails are jerking
round and round
the mill is working:
but when there's no wind —
why, then
I must idle be
again.

Four Scarlet Berries

Four scarlet berries
Left upon the tree,
"Thanks," cried the blackbird,
"These will do for me."
He ate numbers one and two,
Then ate number three,
When he'd eaten number four,
There was none to see!

MARY·VIVIAN

High upon
the Hill I stand,
I am the tallest
in the land.
I've four sails
upon my back
to grind your corn!"
says Windmill Jack.

JEAN KENWARD

Poetry Close-up

1. Read the poem, 'The Harvest' by Alice
    Henderson. Can you explain what
    'ripples of the wheat' means?

    Why does she say — 'I always feel
                    That I am eating rain and sun'?

2. In the poem 'Harvests' by Leonard Clark, what is
    a reaper?

3. List all the words and phrases that Katharine
    Tynan uses in her poem 'August Weather' to
    describe the air.

4. From all the harvest poems, make two lists, one of
    all the foods and crops mentioned and one of all
    the animals.

Other Things To Do

We all need food to stay alive.
.... Find out about carbohydrates, fats, proteins and
    vitamins..... why are they important and in which
    foods are they found?

.... Find out about the harvest of the sea .... which
    fish do we eat? .... where and how are they
    caught?

.... What can you discover about the harvest of a local
    factory .... what does it make? .... how is it used?

.... Find out the ingredients and write out a recipe for
    making bread. Perhaps you can make some.

Hallowe'en

"There was a witch, hump-backed and hooded,
Lived by herself in a burnt-out tree."

Hallowe'en is the night before All Saints Day,
or All Hallows. It used to be thought that ghosts
and witches and all the other evil spirits were out
and about on Hallowe'en because they would not
dare to be out on All Saints Day.
In this section you will find some poems about
witches. Read them and think about these questions.

What makes witches frightening?

.... Think of — wailing chants and black cats ....
cackling laughter .... hooked noses
.... wrinkled skin.

Where might you see a witch?

.... Think of — deep dark caves .... desolate moors
.... silent valleys and gloomy forests.

What do witches do on Hallowe'en?

.... Think of — evil curses .... soaring broomsticks
.... shadows in the dark.

If you wish to write your own poem, these words may help you.

hag	haggard	repulsive	weird	foul	wicked
wizard	vile	malevolent	hideous	gaunt	withered
demon	sinister	ghastly	gruesome	eerie	cloak
cobwebs	ghoulish	cauldrons	matted	cowled	brew

Hallowe'en Happenings

Imagine you were invited to a witches'
Hallowe'en gathering. Describe the food and
drink, the games and guests.

Imagine there was a competition to find the best
'Spell' of the year. Write your own entry.

If you turn to page 67 you will find some questions
on the poems themselves and some more things to do.

THE POETRY LIBRARY

from **Hallowe'en**

The wind has hardly wakened.
Yet flapping through the air
Fly shapes with wings and bony things
And form with jagged hair.

Who blows at my candle?
Whose fiery grin and eyes
Behind me pass in the looking glass
And make my gooseflesh rise?

Who moved in that shadow?
Who rustles past unseen?
With the dark so deep I dare not sleep
All night on Hallowe'en.

MARNIE POMEROY

The Ride-by-Nights

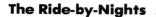

Up on their brooms the Witches stream,
Crooked and black in the crescent's gleam;
One foot high, and one foot low,
Bearded, cloaked, and cowled, they go.

'Neath Charlie's Wain they twitter and tweet,
And away they swarm 'neath the Dragon's feet,
With a whoop and a flutter they swing and sway,
And surge pell-mell down the Milky Way.

Between the legs of the glittering Chair
They hover and squeak in the empty air.
Then round they swoop past the glimmering Lion
To where Sirius barks behind huge Orion;
Up, then, and over to wheel amain
Under the silver, and home again.

WALTER DE LA MARE

from **Mixed Brews**

There once was a witch
Who lived in a ditch
And brewed her brews in the hedges.
She gathered some dank
From the deepest bank
And some from around the edges.

She practised her charms
By waving her arms
And muttering words and curses;
And every spell
Would have worked out well
If she hadn't mixed the verses.

CLIVE SANSOM

Space Travellers

There was a witch, hump-backed and hooded,
Lived by herself in a burnt-out tree.
When storm winds shrieked and the moon was buried
And the dark of the forest was black as black,
She rose in the air like a rocket at sea,
   Riding the wind,
   Riding the night,
Riding the tempest to the moon and back.

There may be a man with a hump of silver,
Telescope eyes and a Telephone ear,
Dials to twist and knobs to twiddle,
Waiting for a night when skies are clear,
To shoot from the scaffold with a blazing track,
   Riding the dark,
   Riding the cold,
Riding the silence to the moon and back.

JAMES NIMMO

Hallowe'en

This is the night when witches fly
On their whizzing broomsticks through the wintry
   sky;
Steering up the pathway where the stars are strewn,
They stretch their skinny fingers to the waking moon.

This is the night when old wives tell
Strange and creepy stories, tales of charm and spell;
Peering at the pictures flaming in the fire,
They wait for whispers from a ghostly choir.

This is the night when angels go
In and out the houses, winging o'er the snow;
Clearing out the demons from the countryside,
They make it new and ready for Christmastide.

LEONARD CLARK

from **Macbeth**

Round about the cauldron go:
In the poisoned entrails throw.
Toad, that under cold stone
Days and nights has thirty-one
Sweltered venom sleeping got
Boil thou first i' th' charméd pot!

Double, double toil and trouble;
Fire burn and cauldron bubble.
Fillet of a fenny snake,
In the cauldron boil and bake:
Eye of newt and toe of frog,
Wool of bat and tongue of dog,
Adder's fork and blind-worm's sting,
Lizard's leg and howlet's wing,
For a charm of powerful trouble,
Like a hell-broth boil and bubble.

Double, double toil and trouble;
Fire burn and cauldron bubble.
Cool it with a baboon's blood,
Then the charm is firm and good.

WILLIAM SHAKESPEARE

The Witches' Ride

Over the hills
Where the edge of light
Deepens and darkens
To ebony night,
Narrow hats high
Above yellow bead eyes,
The tatter-haired witches
Ride through the skies.
Over the seas
Where the flat fishes sleep
Wrapped in the slap of the slippery deep,
Over the peaks
Where the black trees are bare,
Where boney birds quiver
They glide through the air.
Silently humming
A horrible tune,
They sweep through the stillness
To sit on the moon.

KARLA KUSKIN

65

W is for Witch

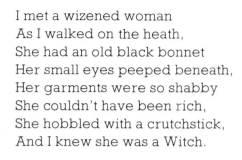

I met a wizened woman
As I walked on the heath,
She had an old black bonnet
Her small eyes peeped beneath,
Her garments were so shabby
She couldn't have been rich,
She hobbled with a crutchstick,
And I knew she was a Witch.

She peered at me so slyly
It made my heart feel queer,
She mumbled as she passed me,
But what I couldn't hear.
I smiled at her for answer
And wished her a good day,
She nodded and she chuckled
And she hobbled on her way.

And so I got home safely.
I didn't drop the eggs,
My nose had grown no longer,
My legs were still my legs,
I didn't lose my penny
Or tumble in a ditch—
So mind you smile and say 'Good Day'
When *you* meet a Witch.

ELEANOR FARJEON

Poetry Close-up

1. Read the poem 'Hallowe'en' by Marnie Pomeroy. What is 'gooseflesh' and what causes it?

2. In 'The Ride-by-Nights', what name is given to the moon and why?

    In the same poem, which words are used to describe different star formations?

3. James Nimmo describes the rise of the witch into the air as 'like a rocket at sea'. What does he mean?

4. What does the word 'ebony' mean in Karla Kuskin's poem 'The Witches' Ride'?

5. Look at the poem 'W is for Witch'. Do you think the 'wizened woman' really was a witch? Give your reasons.

6. Imagine you are a good witch or wizard. Describe a day in your life.

Other Things To Do

.... Find out about Hallowe'en traditions and superstitions, including — lanterns .... apple bobbing .... the carrying of a rowan twig.

.... Hundreds of years ago, how did people test whether someone was a witch or not? Was it a fair test?

.... Read 'The Lion, the Witch and the Wardrobe' by C.S. Lewis.

.... What makes you frightened? Perhaps you could write a poem which lists all the things which frighten you most.

Bonfire Night

"The sky is filled with sparks and flames;
The children rush about."

In this section you will find some poets' thoughts on Bonfire Night. Read the poems and think about these questions.

Why does Bonfire Night make you excited?

.... Think of — blazing branches .... shooting flames .... dancing sparks .... pungent smoke .... soaring rockets .... whirling colours.

.... Think of — crackling wood .... whines and screeches .... exploding stars .... people shouting .... children's laughter.

What do we do for Bonfire Night?

.... Think of — collecting wood .... making Guys .... wrapping up warm .... keeping pets indoors .... enjoying bonfire food.

If you wish to write your own poem, these words may help you.

brilliant	kaleidoscope	crimson	splutter	embers	flare
dazzle	glow	flash	bangs	zoom	flicker
illuminate	gleam	burst	singed	burnt	hiss
fiery	floodlit	arc	scorched	radiant	

Famous Fires

Samuel Pepys wrote in his diary of September 2nd, 1666—

"Jane called us up about three in the morning to tell us of a great fire they saw in the City."

.... Of which city was he writing?

.... Where did the fire start? .... why did it spread so quickly? .... how was it fought and finally stopped?

If you turn to page 73 you will find some questions on the poems themselves and some more things to do.

Fireworks

Zooming, whirring, whizzing round,
Fireworks raining on the ground.
Golden Fountains, Silver Rain
Spurting high — then down again.

Gold and silver in the air;
Don't stand close and do take care.
Tomato soup and chestnuts brown,
Bangers jumping up and down.

ELIZABETH CLARE

Bonfire

There's a great wild beast in my garden
    roaring and surging,
grinding his fierce, gold teeth
    under the trees
where the ground is crinkled and quilted
    with last year's leaf.

I can see his breath through the branches
    floating and climbing
into the calm, cool sky,
    and now and again
if I watch I can see him winking
    an angry eye.

Glinting and plunging he tears
    old paper and boxes
and swallows them till
    he is hungry no longer
but sleeps in a flutter of ashes,
    his sharp tongues still.

JEAN KENWARD

69

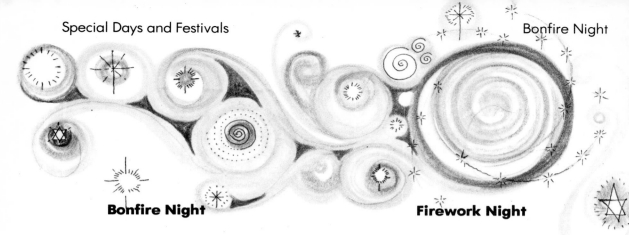

Bonfire Night

All day like a bonfire
The sun is alight
But glows and goes out
In the cold dark night.

The wind makes fireworks
Of the autumn trees
That scatter showers
Of red and yellow leaves.

And I have a bonfire
That like a fiery dragon
Eats the guy
And roars in the garden.

And I have rockets
That shoot up high
With extra stars
To add to those in the sky.

I use my sparklers
To write my name
And the fireworks paint the night
With coloured flames.

STANLEY COOK

Firework Night

The sky is filled with sparks and flames;
the children rush about,
their cries are hardly heard among
the din of bangers, jumping jacks and rockets.

Dogs howl and cats cry—
Frightened of the noise.
The sky is filled with cordite smoke.
The fire is burning high.
Flashes here and crackles there.
A rocket soars into the sky.

Among all this noise nobody hears
a small child sobbing in the shade,
a banger exploded in his hand
and only he can feel the pain.

ERIC SIMPSON

70

Fireworks

They rise like sudden fiery flowers
That burst upon the night,
Then fall to earth in burning showers
Of crimson, blue and white.

Like buds too wonderful to name,
Each miracle unfolds,
And catherine-wheels begin to flame
Like whirling marigolds.

Rockets and Roman candles make
An orchard of the sky,
Whence magic trees their petals shake
Upon each gazing eye.

JAMES REEVES

Fireworks

The rockets soar into the night,
The coloured stars through silver plumes
Fall to a rustle of delight;
And now a waterfall illumes
Excited faces, watching where
In darkness moves a burning brand.
A fountain flares into the air
Like magic from an unseen hand.
Giant catherine wheels catch fire, revolve
In splendour, birds of paradise
Lift rainbow wings, change and dissolve
As the finale rockets rise,
And streaming homewards through the night
That never seemed so dark before,
Our dazzled eyes still hold the light
Of shooting stars that shine no more.

DOUGLAS GIBSON

Please to Remember

Here am I,
A poor old Guy:
Legs in a bonfire,
Head in the sky.

Shoeless my toes,
Wild stars behind,
Smoke in my nose,
And my eye-peeps blind;

Old hat, old straw —
In this disgrace;
While the wildfire gleams
On a mask for face.

Aye, all I am made of
Only trash is;
And soon — soon,
Will be dust and ashes.

WALTER DE LA MARE

The Guy

Dogs break the dust
barking across the dark;
kids, shouting, crack
the air like ice,
ravaging wood or park,
log-laden, against the year's fall.

Shadowing street,
waste plot, or littered yard
they pile their tall
topheavy pyres
of branches, bent and tarred
to burn against this half-remembered ghost

as some straw Guy
who every year must flare
across the night,
fêted in fires,
flame-racked, yet unaware;
lapped in child's laughter endlessly.

ROBERT L. HOLMES

Poetry Close-up

1. In the poem 'Bonfire' by Jean Kenward, what is the 'wild beast' and what are its 'sharp tongues'?

2. In his poem 'Firework Night', Eric Simpson gives two examples of the unhappy side of Bonfire Night. What are they?

3. Read the poem by James Reeves. What do you think the 'magic trees' could be?

4. In the poem 'Fireworks' by Douglas Gibson, what do you think he means by 'a burning brand'?

5. Do you feel happy or sad for the Guy in Walter de la Mare's poem? Can you explain why you feel this way?

6. Read Robert Holmes' poem about 'The Guy'. What do you think he means when he says the children are 'ravaging' woods and parks?

7. Fireworks are very colourful. How many different colours can you find in the poems?

8. Imagine you were a newspaper reporter at the time when Guy Fawkes was arrested. Write a report of an interview with him.

Other Things To Do

.... Write a class letter to your local Fire Station and ask them for some information about fire fighting.

.... Make sure you know all about your school Fire Drill.

.... Make a poster about the Firework Code.

.... Listen to Handel's royal Firework Suite. Can you find out why he composed it?

Christmas

" 'Twas the night before Christmas, when all
  through the house
Not a creature was stirring, not even a mouse;"

Read what the other poets have to say about this
special festival and think about these questions.

What happened on the first Christmas?

.... Think of — no room at the inn .... the baby in the
            manger .... the animals watching ....
            the shepherds on the hillsides .... the
            star .... the wise men's journey.

Why do you enjoy Christmas, at school and at
home?

.... Think of — smiling faces .... festive cards ....
            colourful streamers .... twinkling
            tinsel .... Santa's surprises ....
            Christmas food.

Why can Christmas be an unhappy time?

.... Think of — the old .... the lonely .... the
            homeless .... the sick.

If you wish to write your own poem, these words may help you.

silver	joy	majestic	holly	decorations	lantern
gold	rejoice	goodwill	crib	adorn	candles
crimson	feast	frankincense	mistletoe	manger	reindeer
celebrate	festive	myrrh	stockings	blazing	peace

Christmas Challenge

Can you find out why Mary and Joseph went from
Nazareth to Bethlehem? Draw a map of their route.
What were Nazareth and Bethlehem like at the time?

If you turn to page 80 you will find some questions on
the poems themselves and some more things to do.

from **A Visit from St. Nicholas**

'Twas the night before Christmas, when all through
   the house
Not a creature was stirring, not even a mouse;
The stockings were hung by the chimney with care,
In hopes that St. Nicholas soon would be there;
The children were nestled all snug in their beds,
While visions of sugar-plums danced in their heads;
And mamma in her 'kerchief, and I in my cap,
Had just settled our brains for a long winter's nap—
When out on the lawn there arose such a clatter,
I sprang from my bed to see what was the matter.
Away to the window I flew like a flash,
Tore open the shutters, and threw up the sash.
The moon, on the breast of the new-fallen snow,
Gave the lustre of midday to objects below;
When, what to my wondering eyes should appear,
But a miniature sleigh and eight tiny reindeer,
With a little old driver, so lively and quick,
I knew in a moment it must be St. Nick.

CLEMENT CLARKE MOORE

from **Christmas Landscape**

Tonight the wind gnaws
With teeth of glass,
The jackdaw shivers
in caged branches of iron,
the stars have talons.

There is hunger in the mouth
of vole and badger,
silver agonies of breath
in the nostril of the fox,
ice on the rabbit's paw.

Tonight has no moon,
no food for the pilgrim;
the fruit tree is bare,
the rose bush a thorn
and the ground bitter with stones.

But the mole sleeps, and the hedgehog
lies curled in a womb of leaves,
the bean and the wheat-seed
hug their germs in the earth
and the stream moves under the ice.

Tonight there is no moon,
but a new star opens
like a silver trumpet over the dead.
Tonight in a nest of ruins
the blessed babe is laid.

LAURIE LEE

Silver Bells

Across the snow the silver bells
Come near and yet more near;
Each day and night, each night and day
They tinkle soft and clear.

'Tis Father Christmas on his way
Across the winter snows;
While on his sleigh the silver bells
Keep chiming as he goes.

I listen for them in the night,
I listen all the day;
I think these merry silver bells
Are long, long on the way!

HAMISH HENDRY

Christmas Eve

On Christmas Eve my mother read
   The story once again,
Of how the little Child was born,
   And of the Three Wise Men.

And how by following the Star
   They found Him where He lay,
And brought Him gifts; and that is why
   We keep our Christmas Day.

And when she read it all, I went
   And looked across the snow,
And thought of Jesus coming
   As He did so long ago.

I looked into the East, and saw
   A great star blazing bright;
There were three men upon the road
   All black against the light.

I thought I heard the angels sing,
   Away upon the hill . . . .
I held my breath . . . . it seemed as if
   The whole great world were still.

It seemed to me the little Child
   Was being born again . . . .
And very near . . . . and Then somehow
   Was Now . . . . or Now was Then!

EDNA KINGSLEY WALLACE

The Carol Singers

Last night the carol singers came
    When I had gone to bed,
Upon the crisp white path outside
    I heard them softly tread.

I sat upright to listen, for
    I knew they came to tell,
Of all the things that happened on
    The very first Noel.

Upon my ceiling flickering
    I saw their lantern glow,
And then they sang their carols sweet
    Of Christmas long ago.

And when at last they went away,
    Their carol-singing done,
There was a little boy who wished
    They'd only just begun.

MARGARET G. RHODES

Christmas Daybreak

Before the paling of the stars,
    Before the winter morn,
Before the earliest cockcrow,
    Jesus Christ was born:
Born in a stable,
    Cradled in a manger,
In the world His hands had made,
    Born a stranger.

Priest and king lay fast asleep
    In Jerusalem,
Young and old lay fast asleep
    In crowded Bethlehem:
Saint and angel, ox and ass,
    Kept a watch together,
Before the Christmas daybreak
    In the winter weather.

Jesus on His Mother's breast
    In the stable cold,
Spotless Lamb of God was He,
    Shepherd of the fold.
Let us kneel with Mary Maid,
    With Joseph bent and hoary,
With saint and angel, ox and ass,
    To hail the King of Glory.

CHRISTINA ROSSETTI

The Christmas Party

We're going to have a party
  And a lovely Christmas tea,
And flags and lighted candles
  Upon the Christmas Tree!

And silver balls and lanterns,
  Tied on with golden string,
Will hide among the branches
  By little bells that ring.

And then there will be crackers
  And caps and hats and toys.
A Christmas cake and presents
  For all the girls and boys.

With dancing, games and laughter,
  With music, songs and fun,
We'll make our Christmas Party
  A joy for everyone!

ADELINE WHITE

Poor Decorations

After Twelfth Night
We took the poor decorations down.
I feel sorry for the decorations.
Down comes the holly,
Down comes the ivy,
Down comes the green,
Down comes the mistletoe,
We take the decorations off the tree.
The poor Christmas tree.
It has nobody to dance around it now
It's carried out in the cold.
The Christmas tree is sad
It's stuck in the ground
But the children can please it
By playing around it.
The Christmas tree remembers
That he had silver clothes once.

PETER HANCOCK

Poetry Close-up

1. If you read the poem 'A Visit from St. Nicholas' you will see that the writer 'flew' to the window to open 'the shutters' and throw up 'the sash'.

    What are shutters and what is meant by the sash?

2. Look at the poem 'Christmas Eve' by Edna Kingsley Wallace. Who were the three men and why did they look 'black'?

3. Find another word for Christmas from the poem 'The Carol Singers'.

    In the same poem, how did the listener know that the carol singers were carrying a lantern? What were the weather conditions?

4. In the poem 'Christmas Daybreak' by Christina Rossetti, what is meant by the word 'hoary'?

5. In the poem 'Poor Decorations', Twelfth Night is mentioned. What does this mean?

6. 'I hate Christmas'. Imagine you heard someone say that. Tell their story.

Other Things To Do

.... Who were the wise men and where did they come from?

.... Find out more about the traditions of Christmas, for example, St. Nicholas .... Christmas trees .... holly and mistletoe.